PESACH

A Passover Guide for
Believers in Yeshua

LEX B. MEYER

ISBN-13: 978-1986161671

ISBN-10: 1986161676

DEDICATION

This booklet is dedicated to anyone who wants to become a disciple of Yeshua the Messiah, the Son of God.

CONTENTS

1 WHAT IS PASSOVER..3

2 PASSOVER OR COMMUNION..17

3 PASSOVER GUIDE 25

4 UNLEAVENED BREAD RECIPE...35

ABOUT THE AUTHOR 37

"This is My body which is given for you; **do this in remembrance of Me**."

- Luke 22:19

LEX B. MEYER

1 WHAT IS PASSOVER

Simply put, **Passover is the celebration of our deliverance!** Passover is a Biblical celebration commanded by God in Exodus. It is an annual remembrance of the deliverance that took place in Egypt when God saved His people from slavery in Egypt. We are commanded to keep Passover as a memorial of our deliverance from bondage in Egypt.

> "So this day shall be to you a memorial; and you shall keep it as a feast to the Lord throughout your generations. You shall keep it as a feast by an everlasting ordinance." – Exodus 12:14

Each year at Passover we are commanded to remember how God delivered us from our bondage and affliction. The story of redemption begins in Exodus at the first Passover, but finds its ultimate fulfillment in the Gospels with the blood of Yeshua, the Lamb of God who died for our sins.

> "Therefore purge out the old leaven, that you may be a new lump, since you truly are unleavened. For indeed Christ, our

Passover, was sacrificed for us. Therefore let us keep the feast, not with old leaven, nor with the leaven of malice and wickedness, but with the unleavened bread of sincerity and truth." - 1 Corinthians 5:7-8

Passover reminds us that we have been saved by grace through faith and the blood of the lamb. This is the pattern of salvation we see throughout the Bible. We are completely incapable of saving ourselves, and we lean on the grace and compassion of God to reach down and pull us up out of our bondage.

"For by grace you have been saved through faith, and that not of yourselves; it is the gift of God, not of works, lest anyone should boast." - Ephesians 2:8-9

Passover is often mistakenly referred to as a "Jewish Feast" because it is primarily Jews who celebrate it. However, the Bible portrays it as a celebration for all believers in Messiah, both Jew and Gentile. In fact, I would argue that it is the most Christian celebration we can participate in.

Yeshua (Jesus) and his disciples were celebrating Passover during the Last Supper, therefore many Christians today celebrate Passover to remember the sacrifice of Yeshua, the Lamb of God.

"**Then came the Day of Unleavened Bread, when the Passover must be killed**. And He sent Peter and John, saying, "**Go and prepare the Passover for us, that we may eat**." So they said to Him, "Where do You want us to prepare?" And He said to them, "Behold, when you have entered the city, a man will meet you carrying a pitcher of water; follow him into the house which he enters. Then you shall say to the master of the house, 'The Teacher says to you, "**Where is the guest room where I may eat the Passover with My disciples?**"' Then he will show you a large, furnished upper room; there make ready." So they went and found it just as He had said to them, **and they prepared the Passover**. When the hour had come, He sat down, and the twelve apostles with Him. Then He said to them, "**With fervent desire I have desired to eat this Passover with you before I suffer**; for I say to you, I will no longer eat of it until it is fulfilled in the kingdom of God." Then He took the cup, and gave thanks, and said, "Take this and divide it among yourselves; for I say to you, I will not drink of the fruit of the vine until the kingdom of God comes." And He took bread, gave thanks and broke it, and gave it to them, saying, "This is My body which is given for you; **do this in remembrance of Me**." Likewise He also took the cup after supper, saying, "This cup is the new covenant in My blood, which is shed for you."
- Luke 22:7-20

Yeshua (Jesus) ate Passover with His disciples the night He was betrayed, and He said, "do this in remembrance of me." He was taking the symbols of redemption in Passover and applying them to Himself, showing that He is the true Passover. The events in Egypt were a foreshadow of the ultimate deliverance that would come through Messiah Yeshua. In fact, Paul tells us specifically that the Biblical Feasts are a shadow of the Messiah.

> "So let no one judge you in food or in drink, or regarding a Festival or a new moon or Sabbaths, which are a **shadow of things to come, but the substance is of Christ**."
> - Colossians 2:16-17

Yeshua is the true substance of the Feasts of the Lord, and all of the Feasts point prophetically to Him.

The Lamb

The most important element at Passover is the Lamb. Without the lamb there would be no deliverance. Without the covering of the shed blood of the lamb, we would not have ben spared from death or delivered from bondage.

> "Then Moses called for all the elders of Israel and said to

them, "Pick out and take lambs for yourselves according to your families, and kill the Passover lamb. And you shall take a bunch of hyssop, dip it in the blood that is in the basin, and strike the lintel and the two doorposts with the blood that is in the basin. And none of you shall go out of the door of his house until morning. For the Lord will pass through to strike the Egyptians; and **when He sees the blood** on the lintel and on the two doorposts, **the Lord will pass over** the door and not allow the destroyer to come into your houses to strike you... **It is the Passover sacrifice of the Lord**, who passed over the houses of the children of Israel in Egypt when He struck the Egyptians and delivered our households."
- Exodus 12:21-27

The Bible tells us that Yeshua is the Passover Lamb of God, and His blood was shed for our deliverance. John the Baptist proclaimed that Yeshua was *"the lamb of God"* (John 1:29, 1:36), Paul called Yeshua *"our Passover"* (1 Corinthians 5:7), and Peter said that we were redeemed *"with the precious blood of Christ, as of a lamb without blemish and without spot"* (1 Peter 1:19). The language of Passover is used over and over in the New Testament to describe our salvation in Yeshua. Listen to how Paul describes it in Romans.

"for all have sinned and fall short of the glory of God, being justified freely by His grace through the redemption that is in

Christ Jesus, whom God set forth as a propitiation **by His blood**, through faith, to demonstrate His righteousness, because in His forbearance **God had passed over the sins that were previously committed**, to demonstrate at the present time His righteousness, that He might be just and the justifier of the one who has faith in Jesus." - Romans 3:23-26

God passed over our sins because of the blood of Yeshua. Paul is using the same language that was used in Exodus. He is making a direct connection between Yeshua and the Passover. God sees the blood of the lamb and He passes over us to protect us from destruction.

The fact that God would provide a lamb for salvation was prophesied through Abraham long before the events of Exodus. When God asked Abraham to sacrifice his only begotten son, we see a very profound statement that Abraham says to Isaac.

"But Isaac spoke to Abraham his father and said, "My father!" And he said, "Here I am, my son." Then he said, "Look, the fire and the wood, but where is the lamb for a burnt offering?" And Abraham said, "My son, **God will provide for Himself the lamb** for a burnt offering." - Genesis 22:7-8

We know that God did provide a ram caught in a thicket to take the place of Isaac, but this too was a prophetic picture of the

Messiah. The ram had his horns caught in thorns, just as Yeshua was given a crown of thorns to wear on His head.

Bitter Herbs

We are commanded to eat bitter herbs at Passover to remind us of the bitter affliction and slavery that we faced before our deliverance. It reminds us of the slavery in Egypt as well as the slavery to sin.

> "So the Egyptians made the children of Israel serve with rigor. And they made their lives bitter with hard bondage--in mortar, in brick, and in all manner of service in the field. All their service in which they made them serve was with rigor." – Exodus 1:13-14

The bitter herbs remind us of our sins and afflictions, but Passover reminds us of our deliverance from those things that once held us captive.

> "knowing this, that our old man was crucified with Him, that the body of sin might be done away with, that we should no longer be slaves of sin... Likewise you also, reckon yourselves to be dead indeed to sin, but alive to God in Christ Jesus our Lord. Therefore do not let sin reign in your mortal body, that you should obey it in its lusts. And do not present your

members as instruments of unrighteousness to sin, but present yourselves to God as being alive from the dead, and your members as instruments of righteousness to God." – Romans 6:6,11-13

We rejoice because we are no longer slaves, we have been set free, and have become heirs of the promise.

"Therefore you are no longer a slave but a son, and if a son, then an heir of God through Christ." – Galatians 4:7

Unleavened Bread

During Passover and the Feast of Unleavened bread we are commanded to remove the leaven from our homes and to eat unleavened bread for seven days.

"In the first month, on the fourteenth day of the month at evening, you shall eat unleavened bread, until the twenty-first day of the month at evening. For seven days no leaven shall be found in your houses, since whoever eats what is leavened, that same person shall be cut off from the congregation of Israel, whether he is a stranger or a native of the land. You shall eat nothing leavened; in all your dwellings you shall eat unleavened bread." – Exodus 12:18-20

Before Passover begins, make sure you have removed the

leaven from your home. A lump of dough will naturally become leavened when given enough time to decay. It is a natural fermentation process that takes place. However, leaven is considered to be a corrupting influence on that which is pure. Leaven is caused by decay and aging, and the removal of leaven reminds us to beware of spiritual decay that will corrupt and sour our lives.

Leaven causes the bread to rise and puff up, that is why it is associated with pride, while unleavened bread is called the *"bread of affliction"* or the *"bread of humility."* We need to get rid of our pride and have a humble attitude as we enter the Passover season.

> "Your boasting is not good. Do you not know that a little leaven leavens the whole lump? Therefore purge out the old leaven, that you may be a new lump, since you truly are unleavened. For indeed Christ, our Passover, was sacrificed for us. Therefore let us keep the feast, not with old leaven, nor with the leaven of malice and wickedness, but with the unleavened bread of sincerity and truth."
> – 1 Corinthians 5:6-8

Sin and uncleanness have leavening effects on our soul. It spreads like yeast in dough. Hidden sin and hypocrisy cause corruption, and if we do not remove this leaven, it will eventually be exposed. We are unleavened because of what Messiah has done for us, but we must continue to purge out the old leaven so that we can remain unleavened, walking in the salvation and purity that Yeshua has given us.

> "Search me, O God, and know my heart; Try me, and know my thoughts; And see if there is any wicked way in me, And lead me in the way everlasting." – Psalm 139:23

Wine

Wine is a symbol of blood, and reminds us of the blood that was painted over the doorposts of their homes in Egypt. Yeshua also used wine as a symbol of the New Covenant in His blood.

> "Then He took the cup, and gave thanks, and gave it to them, saying, 'Drink from it, all of you. **For this is My blood of the new covenant, which is shed for many for the remission of sins.** But I say to you, I will not drink of this fruit of the vine from now on until that day when I drink it new with you in My Father's kingdom.'" – Matthew 26:27-29

Wine is also symbolic of covenants, specifically the marriage covenant. Remember how Yeshua turned water into wine at the wedding in Cana? Passover is the marriage supper of the

Lamb, and we look forward to the day when we can celebrate it with Yeshua in His kingdom.

> "And I heard, as it were, the voice of a great multitude, as the sound of many waters and as the sound of mighty thunderings, saying, 'Hallelujah! For the Lord God Almighty reigns! Let us be glad and rejoice and give Him glory, **for the marriage of the Lamb has come, and His wife has made herself ready**.' And to her it was granted to be arrayed in fine linen, clean and bright, for the fine linen is the righteous acts of the saints. Then he said to me, 'Write: "**Blessed are those who are called to the marriage supper of the Lamb**!"' And he said to me, 'These are the true sayings of God.'"
> – Revelation 19:6-9

When is Passover?

Passover begins at sunset on the 14th of Nisan (*the first Hebrew month, in the spring, usually around March or April on the Gregorian calendar*) and marks the beginning of a 7 day celebration called the Feast of Unleavened Bread.

LEX B. MEYER

"Therefore purge out the old leaven, that you may be a new lump, since you truly are unleavened. For indeed **Christ, our Passover**, was sacrificed for us."

- 1 Corinthians 5:7

2 PASSOVER OR COMMUNION

First, I want to point out what Paul says in chapter 10 that sets the stage for his statements about communion in Chapter 11.

> "The cup of blessing which we bless, is it not the communion of the blood of Christ? The bread which we break, is it not the communion of the body of Christ?" – 1 Corinthians 10:16

Where did Paul get this language of eating the flesh and drinking the blood of Messiah? Well, he learned it from Yeshua. The gospel of John records a very important saying of Yeshua in which He says that we must eat His flesh and drink His blood if we want to have everlasting life.

> "Most assuredly, I say to you, he who believes in Me has everlasting life. I am the bread of life. Your fathers ate the manna in the wilderness, and are dead. This is the bread which comes down from heaven, that one may eat of it and not die. I am the living bread which came down from heaven. If anyone eats of this bread, he will live forever; and the bread that I shall give is My flesh, which I shall give for the life of the

world." The Jews therefore quarreled among themselves, saying, "How can this Man give us His flesh to eat?" Then Jesus said to them, "Most assuredly, I say to you, unless you eat the flesh of the Son of Man and drink His blood, you have no life in you. Whoever eats My flesh and drinks My blood has eternal life, and I will raise him up at the last day. For My flesh is food indeed, and My blood is drink indeed. He who eats My flesh and drinks My blood abides in Me, and I in him. As the living Father sent Me, and I live because of the Father, so he who feeds on Me will live because of Me. This is the bread which came down from heaven--not as your fathers ate the manna, and are dead. He who eats this bread will live forever." – John 6:47-58

These are some very significant statements that Yeshua made that we need to pay close attention to, because He said we must eat His flesh and drink His blood if we want eternal life. What was He talking about? How do we eat His flesh and drink His blood? This is the context for what Paul says in 1 Corinthians chapter 11.

"Therefore when you come together in one place, it is not to eat the Lord's Supper. For in eating, each one takes his own supper ahead of others; and one is hungry and another is drunk. What! Do you not have houses to eat and drink in? Or do you despise the church of God and shame those who have

nothing? What shall I say to you? Shall I praise you in this? I do not praise you. For I received from the Lord that which I also delivered to you: that the Lord Jesus on the same night in which He was betrayed took bread; and when He had given thanks, He broke it and said, "Take, eat; this is My body which is broken for you; do this in remembrance of Me." In the same manner He also took the cup after supper, saying, "This cup is the new covenant in My blood. This do, as often as you drink it, in remembrance of Me." For as often as you eat this bread and drink this cup, you proclaim the Lord's death till He comes. Therefore whoever eats this bread or drinks this cup of the Lord in an unworthy manner will be guilty of the body and blood of the Lord. But let a man examine himself, and so let him eat of the bread and drink of the cup. For he who eats and drinks in an unworthy manner eats and drinks judgment to himself, not discerning the Lord's body."
– 1 Corinthians 11:20-29

Notice the somber self-reflection that Paul is encouraging concerning this special meal. When we take this bread and wine, we are partaking in the body and blood of Messiah. This was not a wafer and a thimble of juice. They were breaking bread and drinking wine. We know this because Paul scolds them for getting drunk and full instead of sharing together with the assembly.

Now, the next question we need to answer is how often should we eat the Lord's Supper? The Catholics teach that Eucharist is to be eaten every week during their weekly Mass. Many protestant churches serve communion quarterly. But, what does the Bible say about when we should eat the Lord's Supper? We need to go to the source, and see when Yeshua said to celebrate His memorial supper.

> "Then came **the Day of Unleavened Bread, when the Passover must be killed**. And He sent Peter and John, saying, '**Go and prepare the Passover for us, that we may eat**.' So they said to Him, 'Where do You want us to prepare?' And He said to them, 'Behold, when you have entered the city, a man will meet you carrying a pitcher of water; follow him into the house which he enters. Then you shall say to the master of the house, "The Teacher says to you, '**Where is the guest room where I may eat the Passover with My disciples?**'" Then he will show you a large, furnished upper room; there make ready.' So they went and found it just as He had said to them, **and they prepared the Passover**. When the hour had come, He sat down, and the twelve apostles with Him. Then He said to them, "**With fervent desire I have desired to eat this Passover with you before I suffer**; for I say to you, I will no longer eat of it until it is fulfilled in the kingdom of God." Then He took the cup, and gave thanks, and said, "Take this and divide it among yourselves; for I say to

you, I will not drink of the fruit of the vine until the kingdom of God comes." And He took bread, gave thanks and broke it, and gave it to them, saying, "This is My body which is given for you; do this in remembrance of Me." Likewise He also took the cup after supper, saying, "This cup is the new covenant in My blood, which is shed for you." – Luke 22:7-20

The Lord's Supper that He ate with His disciples was Passover. The bread He broke was Unleavened bread, and the wine they drank was Passover wine. This was the covenant renewal meal that He ate with His disciples. The first Passover was the covenant that God made with Israel in Egypt, and Yeshua renewed that covenant on Passover with His disciples. Then He instructed us to eat Passover in remembrance of Him each year.

"Therefore purge out the old leaven, that you may be a new lump, since you truly are unleavened. **For indeed Christ, our Passover, was sacrificed for us. Therefore let us keep the feast**, not with old leaven, nor with the leaven of malice and wickedness, but with the unleavened bread of sincerity and truth." – 1 Corinthians 5:7-8

I want to encourage you, as Paul did, to keep Passover and the Feast of Unleavened Bread as a memorial to Yeshua in the same way Yeshua taught His disciples.

"**Therefore let us keep the Feast**, not with old leaven, nor with the leaven of malice and wickedness, but with the unleavened bread of sincerity and truth."

- 1 Corinthians 5:8

LEX B. MEYER

3 PASSOVER GUIDE

1. The Blessings as we begin

(Some people choose to light candles at this time)

"Blessed are you LORD our God, King Eternal, who has sanctified us with your commandments and has commanded us to keep the Passover. We thank you for your deliverance and salvation as we remember your Passover. Amen"

(Pour the first cup of wine, the cup of sanctification)

"Blessed are you LORD our God, King Eternal, who creates the fruit of the vine. We thank you for keeping us alive, sustaining us, and bringing us to this season. Sanctify us by your Word, and by the blood of the Lamb. Amen"

Wine represents blood and reminds us of the shed blood that sanctifies us.

(Drink the cup of sanctification)

2. Eating bitter herbs

The bitter herbs (*such as parsley, kale, horseradish, etc.*) remind us of the bitterness of slavery in Egypt as well as the bitterness of sin.

> "Blessed are you LORD our God, King Eternal, who has sanctified us by your commandments and commanded us to eat bitter herbs. Amen"

Take a bite of the bitter herbs *(some people may prefer to eat it on a piece of unleavened bread)*

3. Washing with water

Everyone should wash their hands with water. This symbolic act of purification prepares us to enter into the holiness of the feast. It also reminds us of the red sea crossing, and of our baptism in Yeshua.

(Some may also choose to do a foot washing to follow the example of what Yeshua did with His disciples)

4. Breaking Unleavened Bread

Unleavened bread was used by Yeshua to represent His broken body. We break a piece of unleavened bread and select the best piece and wrap it in a cloth, and place it under a pillow to represent His death and burial, and later we will resurrect this piece as the culmination of our Passover.

5. The Cup of Instruction

(Pour the second cup of wine, the cup of instruction)

It is time to tell the story of Passover. Some choose to read it directly out of the Bible, while others choose to paraphrase it in their own words.

Below are a list of points to cover:

- Israel became slaves in Egypt

- Pharaoh ordered that all Hebrew male babies be killed

- Moses was saved from death as a baby and grew up in Pharaoh's house

- God sent Moses to ask Pharaoh to let the people go

- Pharaoh hardened his heart and God sent 10 judgments on Egypt (*blood, frogs, gnats, flies, diseased cattle, boils, hail, locusts, darkness, and death of the firstborn*)

- The blood of the lamb was placed on the doorposts to

protect them from the destroyer

- The people were set free from Egypt and began their journey

- Pharaoh changed his mind and chased them to the red sea where Israel crossed over on dry land, but Pharaoh and his army were washed away

- Then God gave them His commandments for how to live as redeemed people in His kingdom

- Some people began worshipping idols and were killed for it, some people grumbled and wanted to return to Egypt, and they all ended up wandering in the wilderness for 40 years because of their lack of faith

(Drink the cup of instruction)

6. Eat the Passover meal

Unleavened bread is known as the "bread of affliction", the "bread of humility", and the "bread of haste". We are commanded to eat unleavened bread at Passover to remind us of the bread our forefathers ate when they came out of Egypt. We are also commanded to eat this bread in memory of the death of Yeshua.

"Therefore purge out the old leaven, that you may be a new lump, since you truly are unleavened. For indeed Christ, our Passover, was sacrificed for us. Therefore let us keep the feast, not with old leaven, nor with the leaven of malice and wickedness, but with the unleavened bread of sincerity and truth." - 1 Corinthians 5:7-8

(Take a piece of unleavened bread and break it and say the blessing.)

"Blessed are you LORD our God, King Eternal, who has given us bread to eat.

Blessed are you LORD our God, King Eternal, who has sanctified us with your commandments and has commanded us to eat unleavened bread. Amen"

(Everyone eat a piece of unleavened bread.)

Now it is time to celebrate and enjoy the meal that is set before you.

(Eat your supper and enjoy the fellowship.)

7. The Bread and Cup of Redemption

After supper has ended, we resurrect the piece of unleavened bread that was buried under the pillow. This piece will be used in the memorial of our Messiah.

"For I received from the Lord that which I also delivered to

you: that the Lord Jesus on the same night in which He was betrayed took bread; and when He had given thanks, He broke it and said, 'Take, eat; this is My body which is broken for you; do this in remembrance of Me.'"
– 1 Corinthians 11:23-24

(Take the bread and say the blessing)

"Blessed are you LORD our God, King Eternal, who has given us the true bread from heaven in our Messiah Yeshua. We remember His death, burial, and resurrection. Amen"

(Break the bread and share it with everyone)

(Pour the third cup of wine, the cup of redemption)

"In the same manner He also took the cup after supper, saying, "This cup is the new covenant in My blood. This do, as often as you drink it, in remembrance of Me."
– 1 Corinthians 11:25

(Take the wine and say the blessing)

"Blessed are you LORD our God, King Eternal, who has redeemed us from slavery and sin and given us the way of salvation through Messiah Yeshua. We know that without the shedding of blood there is no forgiveness, and we remember the blood of the Lamb. Amen"

(Drink from the cup of redemption and share it with everyone)

> "For as often as you eat this bread and drink this cup, you proclaim the Lord's death till He comes. Therefore whoever eats this bread or drinks this cup of the Lord in an unworthy manner will be guilty of the body and blood of the Lord. But let a man examine himself, and so let him eat of the bread and drink of the cup. For he who eats and drinks in an unworthy manner eats and drinks judgment to himself, not discerning the Lord's body." – 1 Corinthians 11:26-29

8. The cup of praise

(Pour the fourth cup of wine, the cup of praise)

This cup reminds us of the wedding supper of the Lamb that will take place when Messiah returns. Yeshua told His disciples that He would not drink of the fruit of the vine again until He drinks it in His Kingdom. So, we drink the cup of praise with eager expectation for His return, and we pray for His kingdom to come soon.

(Drink the cup of praise and rejoice. This is also a good time to sing a song of praise, or read a Psalm of praise)

(End the evening with prayer.)

LEX B. MEYER

"You shall eat nothing leavened; in all your dwellings **you shall eat unleavened bread**."

- Exodus 12:20

4 UNLEAVENED BREAD RECIPE

Yield: 6 cookie sheets full

Ingredients:

- ¼ cup oil
- ¼ cup honey
- 2 teaspoons salt
- 3 eggs
- 1 ½ cups water
- 6 to 6 ½ cups bread flour (or all-purpose flour)

Instructions:

1. In a large mixing bowl*, combine the oil, honey, salt, eggs, and water. Stir until well-mixed. Stir in about 4 cups of the flour, then add more flour as needed, and knead into a fairly stiff dough.

2. Divide the dough into 3 pieces. On a lightly floured surface, roll each piece into a large rectangle. You can make them as thin or as thick as you like. (We like ours rolled fairly thin, like a pie crust)

3. Cut rolled dough into squares. (a pizza cutter works well) Place squares onto lightly greased baking sheets. Prick with a fork. Sprinkle with salt if desired.

4. Bake in a preheated 375-degree oven. Bake for 10-20 minutes depending on the thickness of your bread. (Thin dough bakes faster than thick dough). It should be lightly brown on top (do not over-bake or it will be hard and not very good)

5. Remove unleavened bread from baking sheet and place on wire rack to cool, covered with a clean towel. Store in airtight container or bag.

ABOUT THE AUTHOR

Lex Meyer is the founder of UNLEARN, an online ministry that focuses on seeking the truth and exposing the lies we have inherited. He has a degree in Theology, and has devoted most of his life to studying and teaching the Bible. He is also the Pastor at the Grafted Church in Yukon, Oklahoma.

19660976R00027

Printed in Great Britain
by Amazon